REFLECTIONS FOR CELEBRATING MARY'S FEAST DAYS

Rev. Warren J. Savage
and Mary Ann McSweeny

Liguori

ONE LIGUORI DRIVE
LIGUORI MO 63057-9999

Imprimi Potest:
Thomas D. Picton, C.Ss.R.
Provincial, Denver Province
The Redemptorists

ISBN 978-0-7648-1792-2
© 2009 Liguori Publications
Printed in the United States of America
13 12 10 11 09   5 4 3 2 1

Liguori Publications, a nonprofit corporation, is an apostolate
of the Redemptorists. To learn more about the Redemptorists,
visit Redemptorists.com.

To order, call 800-325-9521.
www.liguori.org

REFLECTIONS FOR CELEBRATING MARY'S FEAST DAYS

*Rev. Warren J. Savage
and Mary Ann McSweeny*

The Blessed Virgin Mary is a gift from God in the Church. She was chosen to play an important role in the unfolding of God's universal plan of salvation for humankind. She holds a special place in the hearts of many people and is honored in many nations and cultures under many names and titles throughout the world. Her universal appeal is a sign of her influence in our understanding of the nature of the Church and the meaning of Christian discipleship. She is always viewed as the person who has the most intimate relationship with Christ and someone who helps us in the spiritual life.

Mary's unique relationship with Christ reminds us that the Church is always caught up in the mystery of Christ, and the members of the Church of Christ must walk with an attitude of trust. Mary is considered to be the first disciple, because she listened to the Word of God and acted upon it. Her example challenges us to examine anew the relationship of the Church with the Word—both in an attitude of prayerful listening and in generosity of commitment to the mission of Jesus and the proclamation of the Gospel throughout the world.

Mary is remembered throughout the liturgical year with particular feast days and memorials. This collection of universal reflections focuses on Mary in the context of the Church's liturgical cycle. Selected passages from the Hebrew Scriptures and New Testament serve as the source and foundation of these Marian meditations. The Scripture passages shed light on Mary's role in the history of salvation and her uniqueness as a woman of faith, hope, and love. The reflections and prayers are introduced by particular titles attributed to Mary in the history and tradition of the Church. The titles reflect the Church's evolving understanding of the person and life of Mary in relation to Christ and the Church down through the centuries.

These meditations are intended to help people understand what it means to be an authentic Christian disciple in these challenging times and to inspire all Christians to follow in the example of Mary: to be more receptive to the Word of God, to be more contemplative, and to become proactive in the work of justice and peace in the world. These universal meditations not only honor Mary, but also praise the greatness of the Lord who is always present in the life of the Church and in the hearts of all Christian believers.

MARY,
CHOSEN DAUGHTER OF ISRAEL

...and Eliud the father of Eleazar, and Eleazar the father of Matthan, and Matthan the father of Jacob, and Jacob the father of Joseph the husband of Mary, of whom Jesus was born, who is called the Messiah (Matthew 1:15-16).

Reflection: Generation after generation, God calls the human family to follow in the path of peace and love. As members of God's family, each of us has a special place in this lineage of hope.

Prayer: Lord, Mary carried your hope and love to a new generation. Help me to share your hope and love with everyone I meet.

Mary, Chosen Daughter of Israel, pray for us.

MARY AND THE ANNUNCIATION OF THE LORD

Therefore the Lord himself will give you a sign. Look, the young woman is with child and shall bear a son, and shall name him Immanuel (Isaiah 7:14).

Reflection: Each of us is called to be a sign of God's presence in the world. We know that God is with us when we bear the gift of love, peace, and compassion throughout the day.

Prayer: Lord, you created me to be a living sign of your presence in the world. Give me the grace to bear witness to the reality of your love and peace in all my relationships.

Mary, Favored Daughter of God, pray for us.

THE VISITATION OF MARY

The Lord, your God, is in your midst, a warrior who gives victory (Zephaniah 3:17a).

Reflection: We search for God everywhere. Yet God is right here, in the center of our being, deep in our hearts. We must learn to still the chatter of our minds and sit in quiet to listen for God's voice and loving direction.

Prayer: Lord, you were the center of Mary's life. May you be the center of all my thoughts and actions today.

Mary, visitor to all in need, pray for us.

IMMACULATE CONCEPTION

…"Blessed are you among women, and blessed is the fruit of your womb" (Luke 1:42).

Reflection: All Christians are called to a life of holiness. Our world is made holy when our thoughts and actions come from a pure heart of love and compassion.

Prayer: Lord, Mary was chosen to be the pure vessel of the Savior of the world. Prepare my heart to receive your Word and bear the fruit of holiness in the world.

Mary, conceived without sin, pray for us.

OUR LADY OF GUADALUPE, PATRONESS OF THE AMERICAS

And Mary said, "My soul magnifies the Lord, and my spirit rejoices in God my Savior, for he has looked with favor on the lowliness of his servant...." (Luke 1:47-48).

Reflection: When we truly accept God's presence in the people of every race and culture, then we will be able to eradicate all forms of prejudice and hatred in our homes, workplaces, communities, and world.

Prayer: Lord, Mary's love did not diminish in oppressive times. Help me not to oppress others by my fear and prejudice.

Mary, Our Lady of Guadalupe, pray for us.

MARY, MOTHER OF GOD

But when the fullness of time had come, God sent his Son, born of a woman, born under the law, in order to redeem those who were under the law, so that we might receive adoption as children (Galatians 4:4-5).

Reflection: We feel more secure when things are going according to our plans and time schedule. We have a more difficult time discerning and working in God's time and in accordance with God's divine plan for us.

Prayer: Lord, Mary was chosen to fulfill God's plan in the world. Give me the wisdom to discern and fulfill your purpose in my life.

Mary, Mother of God, pray for us.

MARY, MOTHER OF THE SAVIOR

For a child has been born for us, a son given to us; authority rests upon his shoulders; and he is named Wonderful Counselor, Mighty God, Everlasting Father, Prince of Peace (Isaiah 9:6).

Reflection: In times of conflict, doubt, or indecision, we can turn to the one authority that matters: our loving God. Wonderful, mighty, everlasting, and peace-filled, God holds the solutions to all our problems.

Prayer: Lord, Mary trusted your word. Teach me to ask for and trust your guidance.

Mary, Mother of the Savior, pray for us.

MARY AND THE EPIPHANY OF THE LORD

Then you shall see and be radiant; your heart shall thrill and rejoice... (Isaiah 60:5).

Reflection: We are told that the every person is the face of God in the world. There is little joy and peace in life when our hearts are slow to believe this truth.

Prayer: Lord, Mary saw the face of God. She was radiant and filled with joy. Help me to see your face in all people and be filled with joy and peace.

Mary, pure of heart, pray for us.

OUR LADY OF PROMPT SUCCOR

And the one who was seated on the throne said, "See, I am making all things new" (Revelation 21:5).

Reflection: When the tragedies and disasters of life come upon us, we do our best not to lose faith and hope. With the help of God and a courageous spirit, we can rebuild our lives, our families, and communities.

Prayer: Lord, Mary is a source of strength and hope for your people. She always believed in your power to make all things new. Renew my resolve to face life's disasters with courage and hope.

Mary, Our Lady of Prompt Succor, pray for us.

MARY AND THE PRESENTATION OF THE LORD

...the Lord whom you seek will suddenly come to his temple.... (Malachi 3:1).

Reflection: No matter how often we go to church, pray, or do good deeds, we cannot control God's movement in our hearts and lives. God touches our lives in unexpected ways, in God's own time, and always when we most need it.

Prayer: Lord, Mary's faith gave us a Savior. Grant me the faith to trust you are here and will present yourself at the right moment.

Mary, Mother of Jesus, pray for us.

OUR LADY OF NAZARETH

Then he went down with them [Mary and Joseph] and came to Nazareth, and was obedient to them.... (Luke 2:51).

Reflection: Nazareth was the home where Jesus was loved and cared for. Because of conflicts and wars, many children and youth throughout the world are homeless, orphaned, illiterate, and in need of care.

Prayer: Lord, Mary was chosen to be the Mother of Jesus of Nazareth and the mother of the poor. Open my heart to respond generously to the needs of poor, homeless children in the world.

Mary, Our Lady of Nazareth, pray for us.

OUR LADY OF CANA

Jesus did this, the first of his signs, in Cana of Galilee, and revealed his glory; and his disciples believed in him (John 2:11).

Reflection: God's glory is revealed in simple events. We are witnesses every day to God-events: a beautiful sunrise, the kindness of a stranger, the affection of friends, the care of our family.

Prayer: Lord, Mary knew the great importance of small acts of kindness. May I not overlook an opportunity to show loving kindness to others.

Mary, Our Lady of Cana, pray for us.

OUR LADY OF LOURDES

[The Lord] raises the poor from the dust, and lifts the needy from the ash heap, to make them sit with princes, with the princes of his people (Psalm 113:7–8).

Reflection: It takes complete surrender to God's loving care to be healed of mental, physical, emotional, and spiritual illness. Our inner attitude of willingness allows outer transformation to happen.

Prayer: Lord, Mary's humble attitude made all things possible with you. Heal me of my pride and inner resistance to your loving care.

Mary, Our Lady of Lourdes, pray for us.

MARY, DISCIPLE OF THE LORD

"For whoever does the will of my Father in heaven is my brother and sister and mother" *(Matthew 12:50).*

Reflection: Listening is an act of love. When we deeply listen, we show that we are committed and care about a person. Discipleship means that we are committed to God and listen deeply to the voice of God in our hearts.

Prayer: Lord, Mary listened deeply to your word in her heart and committed her life in service to you and others. Help to discern your will and act upon it in my life.

Mary, Disciple of the Lord, pray for us.

MARY, HANDMAID OF THE REDEEMER

For I am convinced that neither death, nor life, nor angels, nor rulers, nor things present, nor things to come, nor powers, nor height, nor depth, nor anything else in all creation, will be able to separate us from the love of God in Christ Jesus our Lord (Romans 8:38–39).

Reflection: Whoever we are, whatever we do, we are from God, with God, and in God. This is our lasting heritage and covenant.

Prayer: Lord, Mary gave her whole life to you. Show me how I may wholeheartedly serve your people today.

Mary, Handmaid of the Redeemer, pray for us.

MARY AT THE FOOT OF THE CROSS

…Meanwhile, standing near the cross of Jesus were his mother and his mother's sister, Mary the wife of Clopas, and Mary Magdalene (John 19:25).

Reflection: In the midst of personal pain and suffering it is difficult to remain steadfast in faith, strong in hope, passionate with love. We want to deny the reality of pain and run away.

Prayer: Lord, Mary remained a faithful mother in the midst of your pain and suffering. She did not abandon you. Increase my capacity to trust, love, and hope in times of pain and trouble.

Mary, at the foot of the cross, pray for us.

MARY AND THE COMMENDING OF THE DISCIPLES

When Jesus saw his mother and the disciple whom he loved standing beside her, he said to his mother, "Woman, here is your son." Then he said to the disciple, "Here is your mother" (John 19:26-27a).

Reflection: God commends us to the love and care of each other. We are called each day to embody true discipleship by loving at least one other person.

Prayer: Lord, Mary was faithful to your covenant of love. Grant me the faith to follow your way of love and peace.

Mary, Blessed Disciple of the Lord, pray for us.

MARY, MOTHER OF RECONCILIATION

So if anyone is in Christ, there is a new creation: everything old has passed away; see everything has become new! (2 Corinthians 5:17).

Reflection: Our baptism is a constant reminder that in Christ, through Christ, and with Christ, we are made whole and that all of creation is made new. We are forever entangled in Christ's work of reconciliation in the world.

Prayer: Lord, Mary became the mother of reconciliation and the refuge of sinners. Through her intercession, help me to be a loving and forgiving person.

Mary, Mother of Reconciliation, pray for us.

MARY AND THE
RESURRECTION OF THE LORD

But the angel said to [Mary Magdalene and the other Mary], "Do not be afraid; I know that you are looking for Jesus who was crucified. He is not here; for he has been raised, as he said" (Matthew 28:5-6a).

Reflection: There is nothing to fear—not even death. God is faithful to the promise of salvation. We can always trust God's Word to lift us up and give us hope.

Prayer: Lord, Mary witnessed your glory. Let me hear and trust your words of everlasting life.

*Mary, Mother of the Resurrected Christ,
pray for us.*

MARY, FOUNTAIN
OF LIGHT AND LIFE

"I have come as light into the world, so that everyone who believes in me should not remain in the darkness" (John 12:46).

Reflection: The Word of God is the light that guides us in the ways of Christ. The spiritual life remains in darkness when we do not believe what we read, teach what we believe, and practice what we teach.

Prayer: Lord, Mary believed in the Word of God and brought forth light and life for the world. Awaken in me a desire to meditate on and practice the Word of God in my life.

Mary, Fountain of Light and Life, pray for us.

OUR LADY OF THE CENACLE

They devoted themselves to the apostles' teaching and fellowship, to the breaking of bread and the prayers (Acts 2:42).

Reflection: Unity in prayer is a powerful force. We can make a lasting difference by gathering together to pray for peace, justice, and healing in our world.

Prayer: Lord, Mary's whole life was a prayer
and love. Help me to join my voice with oth
praying for peace in our world.

Mary, Our Lady of the Cenacle, pray for us.

MARY, QUEEN OF APOSTLES

*All these were constantly devoting themselves
to prayer, together with certain women, includ-
ing Mary the mother of Jesus, as well as his
brothers (Acts 1:14).*

Reflection: Some cultures, institutions, and organiza-
tions do not honor and respect the gifts and talents
of women. Yet women, too, are made in the image
of God, endowed with dignity, and wisdom.

Prayer: Lord, Mary is held in high esteem and honored in your Church. Remove all forms of prejudice
from my heart that I may treat all people equally.

Mary, Queen of Apostles, pray for us.

OUR LADY OF AFRICA

Because there is one bread, we who are many are one body, for we all partake of the one bread (1 Corinthians 10:17).

Reflection: In Africa, hundreds of thousands of men, women, and children are dying from AIDS. We have a responsibility to care for all the members of our human family, especially those who have no one else to help them.

Prayer: Lord, Mary is mother to all people everywhere. Take away all that blocks me from helping my sisters and brothers who are ill and dying from AIDS.

Mary, Our Lady of Africa, pray for us.

MARY, MOTHER OF THE LORD

And Elizabeth was filled with the Holy Spirit and exclaimed with a loud cry, "Blessed are you among women, and blessed is the fruit of your womb" (Luke 1:41b-42).

Reflection: Each of us is blessed to be a member of God's human family. As we take care to nurture love and peace in our hearts, we have the opportunity every day to be a blessing to others.

Prayer: Lord, Mary gave birth to your peace. Grant me the grace to carry your message of peace and harmony to others.

Mary, Mother of the Lord, pray for us.

MARY, THE NEW EVE

"...See, I am making all things new" (Revelation 21:5a).

Reflection: Hope is a gift from God. For people of faith, it is the promise that our present situation will change and all will become new.

Prayer: Lord, Mary is a sign of hope in the universal church. Renew my heart that I may be an agent of hope for others.

Mary, the New Eve, pray for us.

THE HOLY NAME
OF THE BLESSED VIRGIN MARY

And Mary said, "...Surely, from now on all generations will call me blessed" (Luke 1:46, 48b).

Reflection: God has called each of us by name to be a holy presence in the world. Our willingness to bear the message of God's love and mercy will have great influence on all generations to come.

Prayer: Lord, Mary found meaning in her life by loving you. Help me to know that my only purpose in this world is to be an expression of your everlasting love.

Mary, holy and blessed, pray for us.

MARY, HANDMAID OF THE LORD

Then Mary said, "Here am I, the servant of the Lord; let it be with me according to your word" (Luke 1:38).

Reflection: The only power that matters in the Church and in the world is the power of service. Every member of the Church is called to be a humble servant of the Lord.

Prayer: Lord, Mary is a model of service and discipleship in the Church. Empower me with your Spirit to be a servant of love and compassion for others.

Mary, Handmaid of the Lord, pray for us.

MARY, TEMPLE OF THE LORD

For a day in your courts is better than a thousand elsewhere. I would rather be a doorkeeper in the house of my God than live in the tents of wickedness (Psalm 84:10).

Reflection: Every day we have the choice to dwell in God's temple of peace and compassion. Once we realize the joy and serenity that comes from a day with God, we are less apt to fall back into habits of anger, resentment, and self-pity.

Prayer: Lord, Mary was a temple for your peace. Help me to choose peace over conflict today.

Mary, Temple of the Lord, pray for us.

MARY, SEAT OF WISDOM

But Mary treasured all these words and pondered them in her heart (Luke 2:19).

Reflection: The Word of God is one of the great treasures of the Church. Christians have access to the wisdom of God through reading, meditating, and praying with the Word of God.

Prayer: Lord, Mary treasured the wisdom of God in her heart. Strengthen my resolve to read, meditate, and pray with the Word of God and to seek your wisdom with all my heart.

Mary, Seat of Wisdom, pray for us.

MARY AND THE INCARNATION OF THE WORD

The man named his wife Eve, because she was the mother of all who live (Genesis 3:20).

Reflection: To be fully alive, we all need to experience and embody the courage, creativity, wisdom, and compassion that are associated with womanhood. Holiness comes from wholly integrating these characteristics into our beings.

Prayer: Lord, Mary lived through, with, and in you. Show me the path of holiness, that I may live life to the fullest.

Mary, Mother of God Incarnate, pray for us.

MARY, IMAGE AND MOTHER OF THE CHURCH

On the third day there was a wedding in Cana of Galilee, and the mother of Jesus was there. Jesus and his disciples had also been invited to the wedding (John 2:1-2).

Reflection: Our relationship with God and neighbor is fundamental in the life and ministry of the Church. The whole community suffers when the relationship with God and neighbor is betrayed.

Prayer: Lord, Mary taught us to be faithful to God and neighbor. Help me to be faithful in all my relationships.

Mary, image and Mother of the Church,
pray for us.

MARY AND THE OUTPOURING OF THE HOLY SPIRIT

Sing praise to the Lord, for he has done gloriously; let this be known in all the earth (Isaiah 12:5).

Reflection: God's Spirit pours out an unending flow of forgiveness, mercy, and compassion in our lives.

Whatever our faults, whatever wounds and afflictions we suffer, whatever we have done or failed to do, God's love heals and redeems us.

Prayer: Lord, Mary's whole life was a hymn of praise of your goodness. Bless me with the willingness to witness to your glorious presence in our world.

Mary, touched by God's Spirit, pray for us.

THE IMMACULATE HEART OF MARY

…"You are the glory of Jerusalem, you are the great boast of Israel, you are the great pride of our nation!" (Judith 15:9).

Reflection: The heart is the sanctuary of the Trinity. Every Christian needs to spend more time working on the interior life of the heart. It is from within that the love and glory of God shine forth in the world.

Prayer: Lord, Mary's heart was always attentive and faithful to your will. Re-create in me a pure heart, so that I may be gentle and humble of heart.

Mary of the Immaculate Heart, pray for us.

MARY, QUEEN OF ALL CREATION

"And now, you will conceive in your womb and bear a son, and you will name him Jesus" (Luke 1:31).

Reflection: Each of us is created in the image of God's goodness and love. When we lose trust in our ability to be God-bearers in the world, we need to remember to ask to be shown God's will for us. We can trust that our willingness to be open to God's direction will bear extraordinary fruit in the ordinary events of our day.

Prayer: Lord, Mary gave birth to Jesus the Creator. Help me to witness to God's presence in creation, especially in all your people.

Mary, Queen of All Creation, pray for us.

BIRTH OF THE BLESSED VIRGIN MARY

We know that all things work together for good for those who love God, who are called according to his purpose (Roman 8:28).

Reflection: The meaning and purpose of life is not something we discover in a single moment. It is gradually revealed to us through reading the word of God, discernment, and prayer.

Prayer: Lord, Mary reflected deeply on her call and purpose in the plan of God. Teach me to be more patient with myself as I discern my call and purpose in this world.

Mary, Servant of the Lord, pray for us.

OUR LADY OF THE ROSARY

[Jesus] cried out, "Let anyone who is thirsty come to me, and let the one who believes in me drink" (John 7:37b-38a).

Reflection: We find it difficult to quiet our minds to pray and meditate on the mystery of God. Yet prayer is our true work, and meditation is a renewing drink from the life-giving well of God's mercy, compassion, and love.

Prayer: Lord, Mary played a prayerful role in the mystery of salvation. Strengthen my commitment to pray. Lead me to a deeper awareness of your presence in and around me.

Mary, Our Lady of the Rosary, pray for us.

OUR LADY OF MADHU
(SRI LANKA)

Then Joseph got up, took the child and his mother by night, and went to Egypt, and remained there until the death of Herod....
(Matthew 2:14-15).

Reflection: All over the world innocent people are forced to flee their homes because of war, terrorism, and conflict. Our call is to welcome all who come to our country and communities in search of respite and refuge.

Prayer: Lord, Mary experienced the fear of persecution. Show me how to welcome all those seeking a better life for themselves and their families.

Mary, Our Lady of Madhu, pray for us.

MARY, MOTHER OF GRACE

[Jesus'] mother said to the servants, "Do whatever he tells you" (John 2:5).

Reflection: Life is more hopeful and the outcomes more positive when we work together for the common good of all people.

Prayer: Lord, Mary remained graceful and hopeful through the events of her life. Give me the grace to remain steadfast when I am anxious and upset about many things.

Mary, Mother of Grace, pray for us.

MARY, FOUNTAIN OF SALVATION

"Their leaves will not wither nor their fruit fail, but they will bear fresh fruit every month, because the water for them flows from the sanctuary...." (Ezekiel 47:12b).

Reflection: In the sanctuary of our hearts are the seeds of kindness, compassion, peace, and love. Our mission every day is to nurture these precious gifts and let them flow out to nourish people everywhere.

Prayer: Lord, Mary gave her whole being to you. Show me how to let your love and peace flow from my heart to all those in need.

Mary, Fountain of Salvation, pray for us.

MARY, MOTHER AND TEACHER IN THE SPIRIT

…Maintain justice, and do what is right, for soon my salvation will come, and my deliverance be revealed (Isaiah 56:1).

Reflection: One of the primary duties and responsibilities of parents is to teach their children what is right and to uphold the dignity of every person regardless of race, culture, ethnic background, and way of life.

Prayer: Lord, Mary was a mother and teacher who observed your law of love. May my life witness be an example of unselfish love for all people.

Mary, Mother and Teacher in the Spirit,
pray for us.

MARY, MOTHER OF GOOD COUNSEL

Happy is the person who meditates on wisdom and reasons intelligently, who reflects in his heart on her ways and ponders her secrets (Sirach 14:20–21).

Reflection: It takes wisdom to discern the difference between what we can and cannot change. As we spend time in meditation, we improve our conscious contact with God and learn to change resentment to forgiveness, prejudice to acceptance, violence to peace, indifference to love.

Prayer: Lord, Mary pondered all things in her heart. Open my heart to your wisdom that I may live in peace with my brothers and sisters.

Mary, Mother of Good Counsel, pray for us.

MARY, CAUSE OF OUR JOY

Sing and rejoice, O daughter Zion! For lo, I will come and dwell in your midst, says the Lord (Zechariah 2:10).

Reflection: Joy is another name for God. To experience God's presence in our hearts is to know joy. When we share a joyful smile with someone, we provoke the presence of God.

Prayer: Lord, Mary proclaimed your greatness and rejoiced in your presence. Give me a joyful heart that I may bring happiness and peace to everyone I meet.

Mary, cause of our joy, pray for us

MARY, PILLAR OF FAITH

The Lord is my light and my salvation; whom shall I fear? The Lord is the stronghold of my life; of whom shall I be afraid? (Psalm 27:1).

Reflection: Fear is the absence of love. God's love invites us to accept others and to build strong communities of peace, love, and understanding.

Prayer: Lord, Mary heard your word and followed it. Increase my faith that I may love more and fear less.

Mary, Pillar of Faith, pray for us.

MARY, MOTHER OF FAIREST LOVE

You are altogether beautiful, my love; there is no flaw in you (Song of Songs 4:7).

Reflection: Life reminds us how broken and imperfect we are, but our spirit never stops leading us to perfect love. Deep inside every person dwells the beautiful presence of God.

Prayer: Lord, Mary was chosen to be your perfect dwelling place in the world. Fill my heart with the light of your holiness and make me a dwelling place of your love.

Mary, Mother of Fairest Love, pray for us.

MARY, MOTHER OF DIVINE HOPE

Before the ages, in the beginning, he created me, and for all the ages, I shall not cease to be (Sirach 24:9).

Reflection: Our faith assures us that we are a part of God and dwell through, with, and in God for all eternity. This is the hope that sustains us in times of conflict, sorrow, and spiritual barrenness.

Prayer: Lord, Mary's faith in your word brought new hope to the world. Strengthen my faith that I may bear hope to the hopeless.

Mary, Mother of Divine Hope, pray for us.

MARY, MOTHER OF UNITY

..."He who scattered Israel will gather him, and will keep him as a shepherd a flock" (Jeremiah 31:10).

Reflection: At baptism, all Christians are commissioned to complete the work of God on earth. The mission of the Church is to bring all people to unity in the family of God.

Prayer: Lord, Mary was united with you and your disciples during your ministry on earth. Give me the courage to work tirelessly for greater harmony and peace among all people.

Mary, Mother of Unity, pray for us.

OUR LADY OF MOUNT CARMEL

...[L]ive lives that are self-controlled, upright, and godly (Titus 2:12).

Reflection: Upholding the rights of people who are treated unjustly because of race, gender, sexual orientation, or way of life is a sign of our willingness to honor our God-likeness. Made in God's image of love and goodness, we are each called to love all of our brothers and sisters unconditionally.

Prayer: Lord, Mary intercedes for all who have lost hope. Give me the courage to support and protect the dignity of the poor, disenfranchised, and neglected.

Mary, Our Lady of Mount Carmel, pray for us.

ASSUMPTION OF THE BLESSED VIRGIN MARY INTO HEAVEN

"And blessed is she who believed that there would be a fulfillment of what was spoken to her by the Lord" (Luke 1:45).

Reflection: So much of life and relationships depend on our ability to believe and trust others. It is hard to trust when our hearts have been broken and betrayed by others.

Prayer: Lord, Mary trusted in your word and was given a special place with you in heaven. Increase my faith and trust in your word that I, too, may dwell with you in heaven.

*Mary, Mother and model of the Church,
pray for us.*

MARY, QUEEN AND MOTHER OF MERCY

Then Queen Esther, seized with deadly anxiety, fled to the Lord. She prayed to the Lord God of Israel, and said: "O my Lord, you only are our king; help me, who am alone and have no helper but you" (Esther 14:1, 3).

Reflection: God hears our prayers in joyful times and in times of great anxiety, and responds always with liberating mercy and love.

Prayer: Lord, Mary's being magnified your mercy. Guide my words and actions that I may respond with mercy to all those who hurt me.

Mary, Queen and Mother of Mercy, pray for us.

MARY, MOTHER OF DIVINE PROVIDENCE

As a mother comforts her child, so I will comfort you; you shall be comforted in Jerusalem (Isaiah 66:13).

Reflection: As servants of the Lord, we are called to comfort those who are hungry, thirsty, naked, homeless, sick, and in prison.

Prayer: Lord, Mary was a wise, faithful, loving, and caring mother. May her example inspire me to bring the wisdom and providence of God to others.

Mary, Mother of Divine Providence, pray for us.

MARY, MOTHER OF CONSOLATION

[The Lord] has sent me to bring good news to the oppressed, to bind up the broken-hearted, to proclaim liberty to the captives, and release to the prisoners (Isaiah 61:1b).

Reflection: Blessed are we who have the opportunity to share our plenty with those who have nothing, to listen to and encourage those who are downhearted, and to make friends with our enemies.

Prayer: Lord, Mary took consolation in your championship of the poor and oppressed. Relieve me of my selfish tendencies that I may bring comfort to those in need.

Mary, Mother of Consolation, pray for us.

MARY, HELP OF CHRISTIANS

A great portent appeared in heaven; a woman clothed with the sun, with the moon under her feet, and on her head a crown of twelve stars (Revelation 12:1).

Reflection: We are overwhelmed by the challenges and problems of life. At times, we are afraid and feel all alone in our pain and suffering.

Prayer: Lord, Mary is a model of faithful discipleship. She teaches me how to rely on the strength and protection of God in every trial of life.

Mary, Help of Christians, pray for us.

OUR LADY OF RANSOM

[Mary said], "He has brought down the powerful from their thrones, and lifted up the lowly; he has filled the hungry with good things, and sent the rich away empty" (Luke 1:52–53).

Reflection: We all have the right to be treated with dignity, respect, and justice. No one has the right to abuse or demean another human person. Whenever people are oppressed, terrorized, or victimized, we are called to seek their liberation.

Prayer: Lord, Mary reminds us to lift up the lowly. Grant me the courage to ransom captives of oppression, greed, and injustice.

Mary, Our Lady of Ransom, pray for us.

MARY, HEALTH OF THE SICK

Surely he has borne our infirmities and carried our diseases; yet we accounted him stricken, struck down by God, and afflicted (Isaiah 53:4).

Reflection: Suffering is one of the great mysteries of life. It is difficult to find meaning and purpose in life when we are afflicted with mental, emotional, spiritual, and physical pain.

Prayer: Lord, Mary's acceptance of the Word of God gave birth to the Divine Healer. Help me to accept the Word of God in my life and find health of mind, heart, soul, and body.

Mary, Health of the Sick, pray for us.

MARY, QUEEN OF PEACE

Let me hear what God the Lord will speak, for he will speak peace to his people, to his faithful, to those who turn to him in their hearts (Psalm 85:8).

Reflection: Our prayer life often consists of a one-way conversation: we talk and expect God to listen. Yet true prayer is a dialogue. As we cultivate a listening ear in order to hear God speak, we become at ease with silence and find deep peace.

Prayer: Lord, Mary's heart was open to your word. Open my ears that your word of peace may dwell in my heart.

Mary, Queen of Peace, pray for us.

MARY, GATE OF HEAVEN

And I saw the holy city, the new Jerusalem, coming down out of heaven from God, prepared as a bride adorned for her husband (Revelation 21:2)

Reflection: All of creation is filled with the heavenly presence of God. We must become more aware of God's presence around us and show great care for creation: the earth, the water, the air, and all life.

Prayer: Lord, through Mary the promise of a new Jerusalem was made possible. May the Holy Spirit re-create me to be a gateway of love, peace, and compassion.

Mary, Gate of Heaven, pray for us.

OUR LADY
OF PERPETUAL HELP

…[A]n angel of the Lord appeared to Joseph in a dream and said, "Get up, take the child and his mother, and flee to Egypt, and remain there until I tell you; for Herod is about to search for the child, to destroy him" (Matthew 2:13).

Reflection: There are helpless children all over the world. There are abused and abandoned children, children with AIDS, illiterate children, children dying of hunger, thirst, and disease. We must do more to save the children of the world.

Prayer: Lord, Mary held you close to her heart and protected you from harm and evil. Give me a generous spirit to respond to the needs of children near and far away.

Mary, Our Lady of Perpetual Help, pray for us.

OUR LADY OF SORROWS

Although [Jesus] was a Son, he learned obedience through what he suffered (Hebrews 5:8).

Reflection: In the depth of our grief, suffering, and pain, we can no longer hide behind our mask of pride. We have to admit our powerlessness over the challenges of human life. We acknowledge our dependence on God and let go of our need to be in control.

Prayer: Lord, Mary had many frightening, sorrowful, and perplexing experiences in her life, yet she always trusted in your grace and goodness. Take away the arrogance that prevents me from surrendering my troubles to you.

Mary, Our Lady of Sorrows, pray for us.

MARY, OUR LADY OF KIBEHO (RWANDA)

Then Simeon blessed them and said to his mother Mary, "This child is destined for the falling and the rising of many in Israel, and to be a sign that will be opposed so that the inner thoughts of many will be revealed—and a sword will pierce your own soul too" (Luke 2:34-35).

Reflection: In Rwanda, many people are struggling to overcome the sins of ethnic hatred and genocide. As long as there is hatred in the human heart, and no room for forgiveness, people will suffer and die.

Prayer: Lord, Mary appears to people of all races with a message of peace and forgiveness. Remove all forms of prejudice and hatred from my heart that I may be your messenger of peace and forgiveness.

Mary, Our Lady of Kibeho, pray for us.

OUR LADY OF GOOD REMEDY

He has brought down the powerful from their thrones, and lifted up the lowly (Luke 1:52).

Reflection: It is hard to imagine that in the twenty-first century there is slavery. Young children are taken from their homelands and sold. We need to speak out against all forms of human exploitation.

Prayer: Lord, Mary prophesied that you would come to lift up the poor and the oppressed. Give me the courage to be an advocate of the oppressed and a prophet of justice in the world.

Mary, Our Lady of Good Remedy, pray for us.

PROMISING PRACTICES

- Dedicate ten minutes each morning and evening to sit quietly with the Word of God in prayer and meditation (*lectio divina*). Pray for universal peace, understanding, and peace in the world. Ask the Holy Spirit to help you embody the virtues of love, compassion, peace, and forgiveness in your life.
- Pray the Angelus and the rosary individually, as well as with family and friends. Pray for an end to all wars and conflicts, violence, the abuse of women and children, hunger, poverty, and disease.
- Donate extra clothing and food to a local shelter or food pantry that serves the poor and the needy.
- Practice the disciplines of fasting, prayer, and almsgiving on a regular basis.
- Join a Bible study group to learn more about Mary and her role in the life, teachings, and ministry of Jesus.